D1388998

ULTIMATE TEDDY
B·E·A·R

THE LITTLE BOOK OF

TRADITIONAL BEARS

PAULINE COCKRILL

Introduction by Paul and Rosemary Volpp

DK

DORLING KINDERSLEY
London • New York • Stuttgart

DK

A DORLING KINDERSLEY BOOK

PROJECT EDITOR Polly Boyd
ART EDITOR Vicki James
MANAGING EDITOR Mary-Clare Jerram
MANAGING ART EDITOR Gill Della Casa
PRODUCTION MANAGER Eunice Paterson

FIRST PUBLISHED IN GREAT BRITAIN IN 1992
BY DORLING KINDERSLEY LIMITED,
9 HENRIETTA STREET, LONDON WC2E 8PS

A CIP catalogue record for this book is available from the British Library

ISBN 0-7513-0001-2

Computer page make-up by The Cooling Brown Partnership, Great Britain

Text film output by The Right Type, Great Britain

Reproduced by Colourscan, Singapore

Printed in Hong Kong

Contents

INTRODUCTION

by Paul and Rosemary Volpp

In the late 1970s, British actor Peter Bull appeared on numerous "talk shows" in Britain and the USA saying, essentially, "Look! It's all right for grown-ups to like teddy bears!" He received letters by the bucketful from adults who had rather sheepishly kept their childhood bears packed away for decades! This is how Peter Bull came to be called the "father" of the current teddy bear craze.

Between the covers of this book you will become acquainted with some wonderful traditional bears. What makes a teddy bear "traditional"? The dictionary defines the word "handed down by tradition: conventional, customary". Mathematic designs come to mind as we think of the original, turn-of-the-century teddies. The American Ideal bear is identifiable by its triangular face. Most of the early teddy bear manufacturers repeated this feature to some degree. The early British bears had more of the solidity of a square – they had rounded faces, shorter noses, shorter

EARLY STEIFF
Bruno, a 1909 Steiff bear from Paul and Rosemary Volpp's collection in California.

1950s Bear
A Teddy bear made by Shuco in the 1950s in the US zone of Germany.

arms, larger thighs, and smaller feet. The early French bears we have seen were quite willowy – like French fashion models. They would fit into a narrow rectangular mould. German bears combined many angles. They still reflected Richard Steiff's love of the real bears he sketched so tirelessly at the Stuttgart zoo. They had longer limbs, larger feet, pointed muzzles, and the pronounced hump on the back.

This might be a good time to pass on a recognition tip we received from one of our earliest teachers. Study the features and shapes of teddy bears. Depend more on these features and shapes for identification purposes rather than nose stitching and the number of paw stitches. It is quite likely that the stitching has been redone at some point in time by a clever seamstress, either to make the teddy bear more attractive or more saleable. And it is also possible that the stitching might have been changed to suit an owner's fancy. The body contours – the shape of the head, size of the feet and paws, and proportions of the limbs – are more likely to have remained unchanged.

Key Features
A 1907 American bear displays traditional features – long limbs, large feet, and a pointed muzzle.

TEDDY LONG JOHN

1905 "Last Bear of the Day" Steiff

Centre seam – typical of every 7th bear on the Steiff production line.
No trademark on left ear.
Nose re-stitched with black thread.
Large, original black boot-button eyes.
Holes in original pads reveal that each foot pad has different-coloured felt underlay.
Pale cinnamon-coloured mohair plush.

HEIGHT: 61CM (24IN).

A restorer recently discovered that this particular bear was stuffed with an ancient pair of long johns – a finding that supports the rumour that Steiff used to stuff their bears with rags if they ran out of wood-wool at the end of the day. The different-coloured felt underlay on the bear's feet re-enforces his "last bear of the day" status.

·MARMADUKE·

Pre-World War I British Teddy

Long blonde mohair plush.
Distinct muzzle.
Large, clear glass eyes with pink-painted backs and black pupils.
Nose stitching in green wool – possibly the work of a repairer.
Replacement claws indicated with green wool.
Body stuffed with wood-wool and a growler that no longer works.
Large, woven fabric pads on paws and feet.

HEIGHT: 41CM (16IN).

Although this bear carries no manufacturer's trademark, experts believe that he was made c.1913 by the British company, William J. Terry. This theory is based on an old photograph showing William J. Terry teddies for sale in the London department store, Whiteleys. Marmaduke strongly resembles the teddy bears depicted in the photograph.

WISTFUL

c.1907 Golden Mohair-plush Bruin

Original brown glass eyes with black pupils.
Small, rounded ears sit wide apart on head.
Left eye possibly a replacement.
Fox-like face with sharp, triangular muzzle.
Black thread stitches on nose are the work of a repairer.
Long, curly golden mohair plush.
Long, beige felt foot pads.

HEIGHT: 33CM (13IN).

Wistful was made c.1907 by the Bruin Manufacturing Co. in New York. At the beginning of this century, many firms, such as the Harman Manufacturing Co., Columbia, and Aetna were established in New York to meet the growing demand for Roosevelt-inspired toys. Like these companies, the Bruin Manufacturing Co. was short lived.

WALTZING MATILDA

1930s–40s Australian Joy Toys Bear

Golden-yellow mohair plush.
Nose indicated with black, vertical stitching.
Arms extend the length of the torso.
Embroidered cotton label bearing manufacturer's name stitched on to beige felt foot pad.
Clear glass eyes with amber-painted backs and black pupils.
Unjointed neck – a distinguishing feature of many Australian bears of all ages.
Slightly pointed, upturned paws.
JOY-TOYS
MADE IN AUSTRALIA

HEIGHT: 38CM (15IN).

Joy Toys was established by Mr. and Mrs. Kirby in South Yarra, Victoria, Australia in the 1920s. It was one of the earliest teddy bear makers in Australia (until the 1920s, most teddies had been imported from Britain and Germany), but it was taken over by the British firm, Lines Bros., in the 1960s. The Joy Toys name was used until the 1970s.

P.A. POOH

1930s Top-quality Chiltern Bear

High-quality, soft golden mohair plush.
Black, vertically stitched nose.
Replacement amber and black plastic eyes.
Body-length arms shorter than those of German bears.
Velveteen pads – a distinctive feature of Chiltern bears.

HEIGHT: 51CM (20IN).

Made in the 1930s by H.G. Stone & Co. Ltd., P.A. Pooh is a fine example of a Chiltern soft toy. These were so-called because the toy-making factory was based in the Chiltern Hills of Buckinghamshire, England. With his big thighs and short arms, P.A. Pooh displays the key characteristics of a bear in the Hugmee range of bears.

PARRAMATTA PAUL

Early Brown Mohair-plush Steiff from Australia

Small, black boot-button eyes.
Steiff button with raised lettering in left ear.
Pronounced muzzle typical of early Steiffs.
Body stuffed with wood-wool.
Feet have five claws, whereas paws have four claws.
Long limbs.
Worn brown mohair plush.

HEIGHT: 33CM (13IN).

Parramatta Paul, a small, early Steiff, has spent most of his life in Australia. In 1903, an Australian sea captain bought him in Europe as a present for his daughter. The worn state of his mohair plush suggests that she loved him dearly. His present owners named him after his Australian home town, Parramatta, which is just outside Sydney.

·CLAUS·

1927 Gebrüder Hermann Bear

Front of ear same material as muzzle.
Short-pile cream mohair plush on muzzle.
Brown glass eyes with black pupils.
Black, horizontally stitched nose.
Dual-coloured mohair plush – beige, tipped with rich cinnamon.
Black thread claws stitched across mohair plush.
Small feet with oval, cream felt pads.

HEIGHT: 43CM (17IN).

Stimulated by the teddy bear phenomenon, Johann Hermann founded a firm in 1907 to rival Steiff. Bears from the two German factories can be difficult to tell apart, although the muzzle of a Hermann bear is usually made from a different fabric to that of the head and body. Claus, a handsome teddy, was made by Gebrüder Hermann in 1927.

Big Ben

Chad Valley's Typical British Bear

Large, soft ears in excellent condition.
Large, wide head.
Original amber and black glass eyes.
Compact, vertical stitching on nose – a typical Chad Valley feature.
Arms short compared to those of German bears.
Brown rexine pads on paws and feet. No claws indicated.
Good-grade golden mohair plush.

HEIGHT: 107CM (42IN).

Big Ben is the classic British bear. His big thighs, large, wide head and ears, plump body, rather short arms, and rounded feet make him quite distinct from the German, French, and American bears of the same period (c.1940). His manufacturers, Chad Valley, whose factory was in Shropshire, England, were one of Merrythought's rivals at the time.

AHSOO

1930s Japanese Carnival Teddy Bear

Pinkish orange synthetic plush on knitted backing.
Large, wired ears.
Velveteen muzzle with black, stitched nose.
Original pink ribbon with bell tied at neck.
Arm joints connected by rod, so arms move together.
Stitched claws join up with painted claws on base of pads.
Short, stubby arms with unusually pointed paws.

HEIGHT: 38CM (15IN).

The distinctive painted claw patterns on Ahsoo's foot pads, and the jointing system for his arms, suggest this bear has Japanese origins. He is possibly a carnival bear, who would have been given as a prize at a fair. This particular example resembles Steiff's Teddy Baby – a bear cub distinguished by his exceptionally large feet and a bell around his neck.

Bing Oh!

c.1911 Gebrüder Bing

Dark brown mohair plush.
Original shiny black boot-button eyes.
Hand-embroidered, triangular nose.
Traditional inverted V-shaped mouth.
Mohair plush clipped around muzzle.
Metal button incised "GBN" under left arm.
Large feet with replacement leather pads.
Long arms and curved paws.

HEIGHT: 53CM (21IN).

This handsome brown bear, resembling Steiff bears of the same period, was a product of the German soft-toy manufacturers, Gebrüder Bing. In 1909, Steiff took legal action against this rival company to prevent them imitating the distinctive "button in ear" trademark. As a result, Bing Oh! bears a metal button trademark under his left arm.

CHILLI PEPPER

1940s H.G. Stone & Co. Ltd.

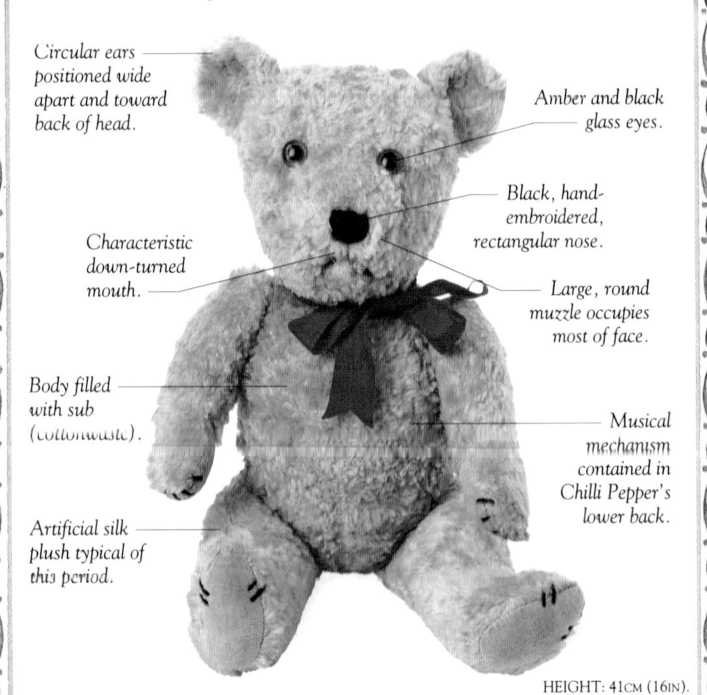
Circular ears positioned wide apart and toward back of head.
Amber and black glass eyes.
Black, hand-embroidered, rectangular nose.
Characteristic down-turned mouth.
Large, round muzzle occupies most of face.
Body filled with sub (cottonwaste).
Musical mechanism contained in Chilli Pepper's lower back.
Artificial silk plush typical of this period.

HEIGHT: 41CM (16IN).

This attractive, coral-pink bear was made by a prominent British toy manufacturer based in the Chiltern Hills of England, and is subsequently known as a "Chiltern" bear. He is a musical teddy, and plays "Brahms' Lullaby" when he is wound up. The clockwork musical mechanism is housed in Chilli's lower back, and is controlled by a protruding key.

ARTHUR

1930s Inexpensive Dutch Teddy Bear

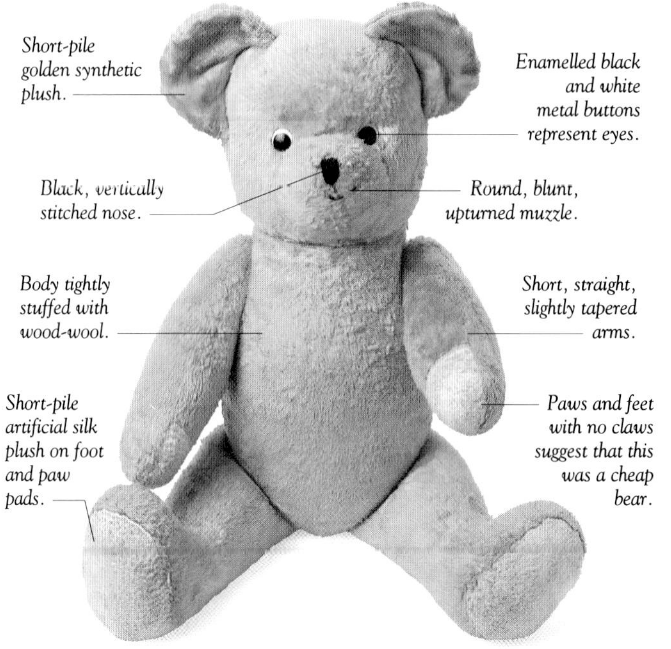

Short-pile golden synthetic plush.
Enamelled black and white metal buttons represent eyes.
Black, vertically stitched nose.
Round, blunt, upturned muzzle.
Body tightly stuffed with wood-wool.
Short, straight, slightly tapered arms.
Short-pile artificial silk plush on foot and paw pads.
Paws and feet with no claws suggest that this was a cheap bear.

HEIGHT: 71CM (28IN).

Although Arthur van Gelden has no trademark, his strong resemblance to other Dutch bears, such as his heavy, compact stuffing, suggests that he was made in Holland. He belongs to a cheaper range of large bears. This can be identified by the absence of any claws on his paws and feet and the artificial silk plush that has been used for his fur.

Gigi

1930s High-quality French Teddy Bear

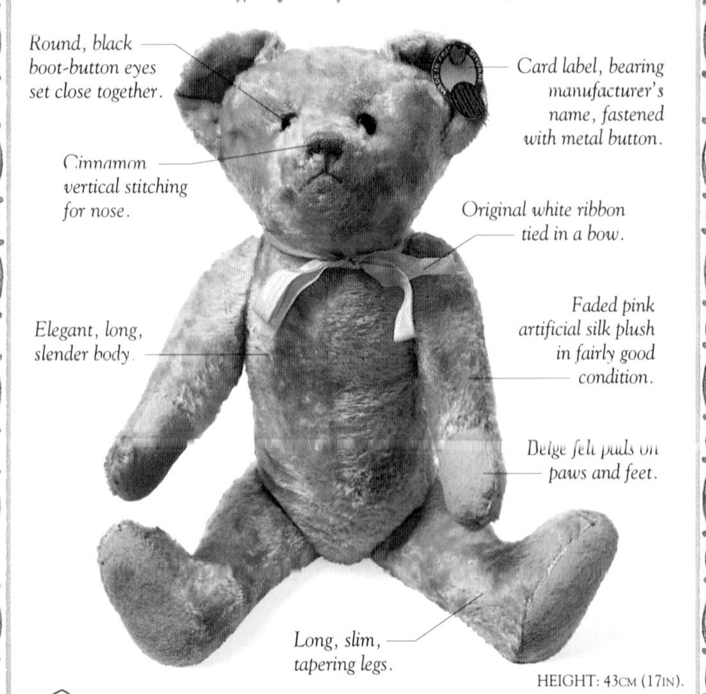
Round, black boot-button eyes set close together.
Card label, bearing manufacturer's name, fastened with metal button.
Cinnamon vertical stitching for nose.
Original white ribbon tied in a bow.
Faded pink artificial silk plush in fairly good condition.
Elegant, long, slender body.
Beige felt pads on paws and feet.
Long, slim, tapering legs.

HEIGHT: 43CM (17IN).

Gigi was made by Fadap, a toy-manufacturing company founded in Divonne, France. Like Maurice, another French bear (*see page 34*), she was made in the 1930s, but she would have been more expensive than Maurice, as she is made of high-quality materials, and has a more sophisticated jointing system (each arm and leg can move independently).

Big Teddy

c.1910 Kresge Family Bear

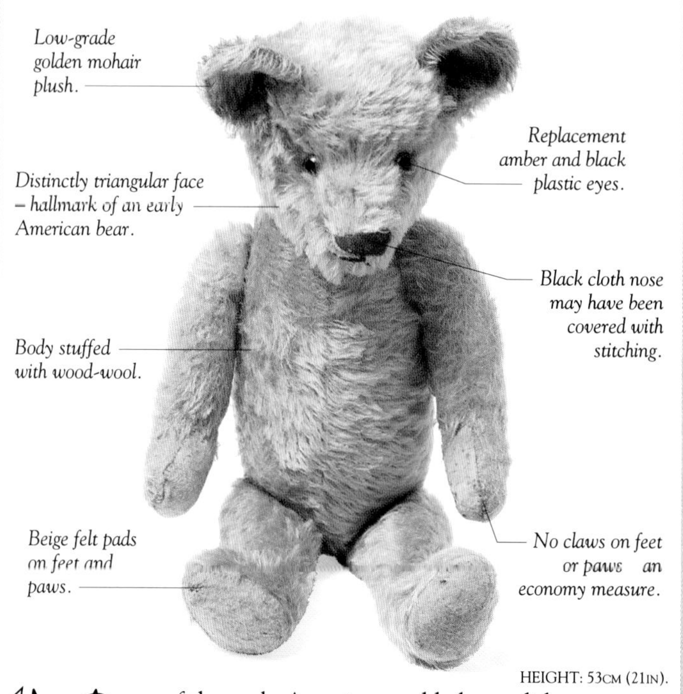

Low-grade golden mohair plush.
Replacement amber and black plastic eyes.
Distinctly triangular face – hallmark of an early American bear.
Black cloth nose may have been covered with stitching.
Body stuffed with wood-wool.
Beige felt pads on feet and paws.
No claws on feet or paws – an economy measure.

HEIGHT: 53CM (21IN).

Many of the early American teddy bears did not carry a trademark, making their identification difficult. The fact that this teddy was made from cheap materials suggests that he is not an Ideal. Until recently, he had spent all of his life in the Kresge family, founders of the Kresge five-and-ten stores, which evolved into the Kmart chain.

LINDY

Buck Hill Collection's First Steiff

Original black boot-button eyes.
Steiff button with raised lettering in left ear.
Black, horizontally stitched nose.
Golden mohair plush in mint condition.
Body filled with wood-wool stuffing.
Four black stitches for claws on feet and paws.
Long, large, narrow feet.

HEIGHT: 31CM (12IN).

Lindy was the first traditional bear bought by Rosemary and Paul Volpp. Today, their Buck Hill collection, which numbers 5,000 bears, is considered the best in the world. The pattern from which this 1905 Steiff was made is similar to that of one of the earliest Steiffs put into production – the Richard Steiff bear that is held in the firm's archives.

·EDDIE·

1903–1905 Blank-buttoned Steiff

Small, rounded ears placed wide apart – a feature of early Steiffs.
Blank, nickel-plated Steiff button.
Black, horizontal stitching on nose outlined by two diagonal stitches.
Small, black boot-button eyes set close together.
Four paws, each indicated with a single black stitch across the mohair plush.
Replacement foot pad.

HEIGHT: 33CM (13IN).

Eddie is almost identical to Lindy (*see opposite*), but for the blank, nickel-plated button in Eddie's ear. Blank buttons were generally used between 1903–1905, before Steiff introduced their name on the button, and prior to registering their "button in ear" trademark. These blank buttons were used occasionally after 1905 in order to use up old stock.

STILL HOPE

1907 Aetna Toy Animal Co.

Large ears placed wide apart across top of head.
Brown and black glass eyes distinguish him from other early American bears.
Triangular nose indicated with black, vertical stitching.
Wood-wool-stuffed body contains tilt growler.
Oval, beige felt pads reinforced with card.
Five black claws stitched across beige mohair plush.
Aetna stamp on left foot pad.

HEIGHT 51CM (20IN).

This early American bear is named after an ancestor of his present owners, who was scalped and left for dead by native Americans. However, the ancestor recovered, and lived to the remarkable age of 110! Still Hope was made by the Aetna Toy Animal Co., one of the many American teddy bear manufacturers established in the early 1900s.

Chummy

1930s Classic Merrythought Bear

Amber and black glass eyes.
Celluloid button bearing firm's name attached to left ear.
Clipped mohair plush on pointed muzzle.
Slightly shaggy golden mohair plush.
Body filled with kapok and wood-wool mix.
Claw stitching on paw typical of Merrythought bears of the period.
Fabric label stitched to right felt foot pad.

HEIGHT 58CM (23IN).

One of Merrythought's earliest creations, Chummy, demonstrates the emergence of Britain's new-style teddy bear with shorter arms, a straight back, and a mix of kapok and wood-wool stuffing. These features distinguish him from the early German and American bears of this period, with their long limbs, hump backs, and wood-wool stuffing.

·PERFECTION·

c.1903 Prototype Steiff

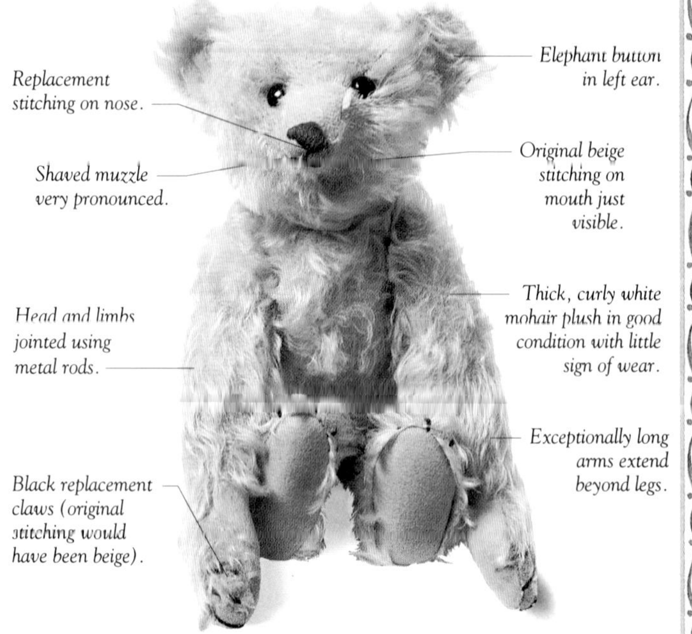

Replacement stitching on nose.
Elephant button in left ear.
Shaved muzzle very pronounced.
Original beige stitching on mouth just visible.
Head and limbs jointed using metal rods.
Thick, curly white mohair plush in good condition with little sign of wear.
Exceptionally long arms extend beyond legs.
Black replacement claws (original stitching would have been beige).

HEIGHT: 38CM (15IN).

Steiff experimented with various prototypes to develop a suitable pattern for production, so many early Steiff bears differ slightly from one another. Perfection is probably one of these prototypes, as she is not like any known production bears. White Steiffs are less common than golden or beige Steiffs, but not as rare as the black models.

M'Lady Briscoe

c.1940 J.K. Farnell

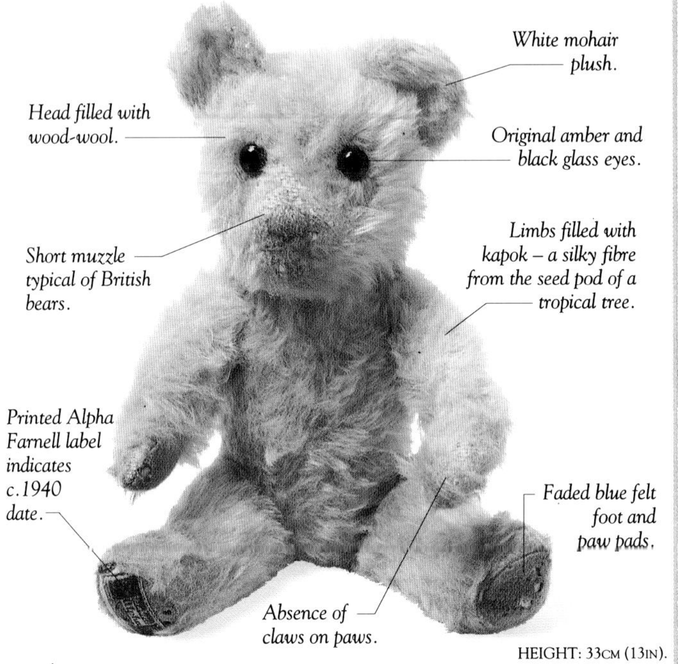
White mohair plush.
Head filled with wood-wool.
Original amber and black glass eyes.
Short muzzle typical of British bears.
Limbs filled with kapok – a silky fibre from the seed pod of a tropical tree.
Printed Alpha Farnell label indicates c.1940 date.
Faded blue felt foot and paw pads.
Absence of claws on paws.

HEIGHT: 33CM (13IN).

The Alpha series was a range of bears patented by the previously London-based company, J.K. Farnell, in the 1920s. Kapok, the stuffing used for this bear's limbs, was preferred by British firms because it is softer, lighter, and more hygienic than wood-wool, and could be bought cheaply from countries within the British Empire.

·Francois·

French World War I Teddy Bear

Black boot-button eyes.
Black, horizontally stitched nose.
Long, lean torso filled with wood-wool stuffing.
White felt pads on paws and feet.
Distinct inverted-V-shaped mouth stitched with black thread.
Blue artificial silk plush – "coloured" bears were becoming increasingly popular by World War I.
Three black, stitched claws on each paw and foot.

HEIGHT: 43CM (17IN).

The first company to make teddy bears in France was Thiennot in 1919, when bans imposed on imports from Germany, the centre of the toy-making industry, opened up opportunities for toy manufacturing to develop elsewhere. These bears were generally tall, elegant, and long-legged compared with their European and American cousins.

DICKIE

c.1950 German Schuco

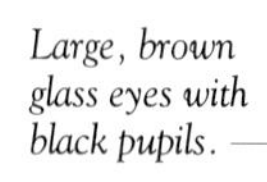

Large, brown glass eyes with black pupils.
Beige mohair plush tinged with pink in good condition.
Down-turned paws – a feature of Schuco bears.
Three black claws stitched across mohair fill-plush.
Body filled with kapok stuffing.
Reverse side of original red plastic trademark reads, "Made in U.S. zone, Germany".
Rounded felt pads reinforced with card.
Schuco TRICKY

HEIGHT: 33CM (13IN).

Dickie's red plastic tag indicates that he is a Tricky teddy – one of a range of Yes/No bears made by the German firm, Schreyer and Co. (often abbreviated to Schuco). These bears all had small tails that acted as levers: by pulling the tail up and down and from side to side, you could make the bears nod or shake their heads.

MR ROOSEVELT SR

1940s New-style American Bear

Golden mohair plush.
Large ears set wide apart – a feature of Knickerbocker bears.
Brown and black glass eyes, sewn into face seams, are possibly replacements.
Short, rounded, clipped mohair-plush muzzle.
Black, vertical stitching for nose.
Short limbs less firmly stuffed with kapok than rest of body.
Beige velveteen pads.

HEIGHT: 51CM (20IN).

This teddy is the creation of the Knickerbocker Toy Co. Inc., an American firm noted for the Smokey Bears they produced in the 1960s and 1970s. Although he was in fact made c.1940, Mr. Roosevelt Sr. is more typical of the flatter teddy bears that dominated after World War II, with his large, rounded head, flat muzzle, straight back, and short limbs.

LOUISE

1921 White Mohair-plush Steiff

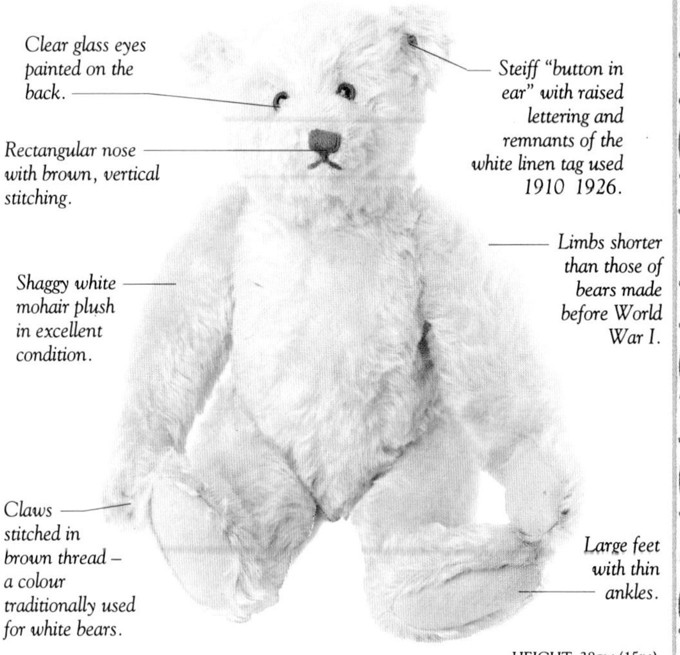

Clear glass eyes painted on the back.
Steiff "button in ear" with raised lettering and remnants of the white linen tag used 1910 1926.
Rectangular nose with brown, vertical stitching.
Limbs shorter than those of bears made before World War I.
Shaggy white mohair plush in excellent condition.
Claws stitched in brown thread – a colour traditionally used for white bears.
Large feet with thin ankles.

HEIGHT: 38CM (15IN).

Certain features distinguish Louise from Steiff bears made before World War I. She has glass instead of boot-button eyes, her limbs are shorter, and she is filled with a mixture of kapok and wood-wool stuffing to make her more cuddly. However, with her protruding muzzle and humped back, she retains the traditional Steiff bear shape.

Gentle Ben

Early American Ideal Novelty & Toy Co. Bear

Triangular face – a feature of early American bears.
Small, black boot-button eyes.
Black, horizontally stitched nose.
Five black claws on paws and feet.
Steiff metal button added at later date to deceive buyers.
Beige mohair plush in good condition.
Feet slightly pointed.

HEIGHT: 28CM (11IN).

The Ideal Novelty & Toy Co. was the first firm in the United States to make teddy bears. Gentle Ben, dating from 1904–1905, is one of their earliest models. Ben's pretty, distinctly triangular face indicates that he is an Ideal bear, even though someone has sewn a Steiff button on his left ear in an attempt to convince buyers otherwise.

·BRUNO·

Good-sized 1909 Steiff

Large, black boot-button eyes.
Steiff button with raised lettering in left ear.
Well-worn, pointed muzzle.
Black thread nose with vertical stitching.
Beige mohair plush slightly worn.
Four black claws on each paw and foot stitched across mohair plush.
Hole in pad reveals felt underlay and wood-wool stuffing.

HEIGHT: 71CM (28IN).

Bruno, a large 1909 Steiff, arrived in the United States as padding around an English family's best set of china. As demand for good-quality Steiffs increased, the English family decided to sell him to a dealer. His present owners, Paul and Rosemary Volpp, paid £2,300 (US $4,000) for him in 1985 – a price that reflects his good condition.

MR FLUFFY

1923 Chad Valley Bear with Aerolite Trademark

Small metal and celluloid button bearing Aerolite trademark.
Glass eyes held on wire shanks.
Long-pile golden mohair plush.
Black claws on paws and feet stitched across mohair plush
Limbs filled with kapok stuffing.
Body, stuffed with kapok and wood-wool, contains broken voice box.
Velveteen oval pads reinforced with stiff cardboard.

HEIGHT: 41CM (16IN).

Chad Valley, a company with a factory in Wellington in Shropshire, England, began specializing in soft toys in 1920 as demand for British bears grew. Manufactured in 1923, Mr Fluffy is one of their first bears to carry the Aerolite trademark. This was used between 1923 and 1926, and indicates that the bear was stuffed mainly with kapok.

OTHELLO

1912 Shaggy Black Steiff Bear

Large ears set wide apart and sewn into facial seams.
Steiff button with raised lettering in left ear.
Black boot-button eyes, each set on an orange felt circle.
Protruding, clipped mohair-plush muzzle.
Long, shaggy black mohair plush.
Long, curved arms typical of early Steiff bears.
Long, narrow pads of beige felt in perfect condition.

HEIGHT: 48CM (19IN).

Othello, a rare teddy bear, is one of only 494 shaggy black mohair teddy bears to be made by Steiff for the British market in 1912. The German firm produced one other model of a black bear in 1907, but unlike Othello, he had red stitched claws, a sealing wax nose, and was without the distinctive orange felt circles that surround Othello's eyes.

Maurice

French 1930s Depression Bear

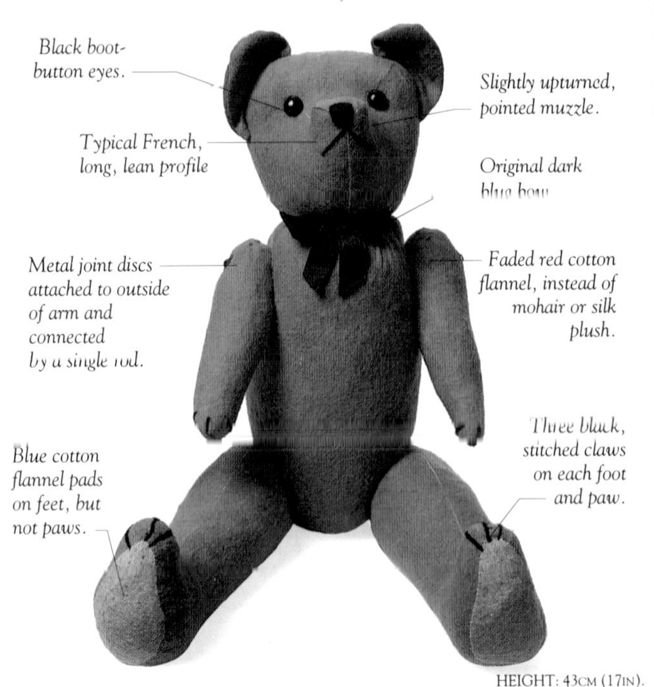
Black boot-button eyes.
Slightly upturned, pointed muzzle.
Typical French, long, lean profile
Original dark blue bow
Metal joint discs attached to outside of arm and connected by a single rod.
Faded red cotton flannel, instead of mohair or silk plush.
Three black, stitched claws on each foot and paw.
Blue cotton flannel pads on feet, but not paws.

HEIGHT: 43CM (17IN).

This unfortunate French bear shows the tell-tale signs of having been made during the Depression. The absence of paw pads, the use of cotton flannel, his short limbs, and a jointing system that only allows the arms to move together (they usually move independently) all indicate that the manufacturer was economizing on materials and labour.

Miss Nightingale

c.1912 British Teddy Bear

Wide, high forehead is typical of British bears.
Small, rounded ears gathered and fitted into seams of bear's face.
Unusual eyes made from round, convex pieces of metal painted black.
Wide, smiling mouth made from black woollen thread.
Arms shorter and straighter than her contemporaries.
Long, thin body and straight back.
Short-pile golden mohair plush.
Small, rounded feet with beige felt pads.

HEIGHT: 48CM (19IN).

One of the earliest of all British bears, Miss Nightingale is thought to pre-date World War I, dispelling the myth that the first bears are either German or American. She is unmarked, so unfortunately her makers are a mystery, but we can see how she differs from her German cousins with her long body, short arms, small feet, and straight back.

BINGLE BILL

Early 1920s Gebrüder Bing

Replacement brown plastic eyes with black pupils.
Black, vertical stitching represents nose.
Orange button trademark on right arm.
Pronounced, closely shaved mohair-plush muzzle.
Long, silky, silver-tipped mohair plush, made specially for the teddy bear industry.
Replacement beige felt pads.

HEIGHT: 58CM (23IN).

The orange button trademark, with the letters "BW" (Bing Werke) attached to this bear's right arm, confirms that he was made after 1919. Bing bears manufactured prior to this date carry a silver-coloured button reading "GBN" (Gebrüder Bing Nuremberg) under their left arm. Bing bears are only rarely found with their buttons intact.

BERTIE

1930s British Teddy Bear

Large, triangular head with wide forehead.
Glass eyes, held on wire shanks, stitched into position.
Wood wool and kapok-stuffed body contains working tilt growler.
Most of pile worn away on paw and foot pads.
Stocky legs with large, stubby feet.
Worn label bearing manufacturer's name.

HEIGHT: 66CM (26IN).

In 1903, Henry Samuel Dean established Dean's Rag Book Co. in Fleet St., London. Originally manufacturers of rag books and printed, cloth cut-out sheets of soft toys, they did not begin to produce plush teddy bears until the end of World War I. When Bertie was made in the 1930s, the company was at the height of its success.

BEAR OWNERS

Dorling Kindersley would like to thank the following people, who generously lent their teddy bears for photography:

• Heather Bischoff
for Marmaduke page 7

• Gyles Brandreth,
from the Teddy Bear Museum at Stratford-upon-Avon in the UK, for Claus page 12

• Pauline Cockrill
for Chilli Pepper page 16

• Pam Hebbs
for Eddie page 21 and Louise page 29

• Ian Pout
for Othello page 33

• Private Collection
for Arthur page 17

• Judy Sparrow,
from The Bear Museum at Petersfield in Hampshire in the UK for Chummy page 23; Mr. Fluffy page 32 and 39; Miss Nightingale page 35 and Bertie page 37

• Paul and Rosemary Volpp
for Teddy Long John page 1 and 6; Gentle Ben page 1 and 30; Lindy page 2 and 20; Bruno page 3, 4 and 31, Dickie page 5 (top) and 27; Wistful page 5 (bottom) and 8; Waltzing Matilda page 9; P.A. Pooh page 10; Parramatta Paul page 11; Big Ben page 13; Ahsoo page 14; Bing Oh! page 15; Gigi page 18; Big Teddy page 19; Still Hope page 22; Perfection page 24; M'Lady Briscoe page 25; Francois page 26; Mr. Roosevelt Sr. page 28; Maurice page 34; Bingle Bill page 36 and 41; and the replica of Happy page 38.

Useful Addresses

The Bear Museum
38 Dragon Street
Petersfield
Hampshire GU31 4JJ
☎ 0730 265108

Merrythought's Shop & Museum
Dale End, Ironbridge
Telford
Shropshire TF8 7NJ
☎ 0952 433029

Bethnal Green Museum of Childhood
Cambridge Heath Road
London E2 9PA
☎ 081 981 1711/6789

Museum of Childhood
42 High Street
Edinburgh
Scotland EH1 1TG
☎ 031 225 2424 ext. 6645

Cotswold Teddy Bear Museum
76 High Street
Broadway
Worcestershire WR12 7AJ
☎ 0386 858323

The Steiff Museum
Margarete Steiff GmbH
PO Box 1560
Alliin Straase 2
D-7928
Giengen (Brenz)
Germany
☎ 010 49 7322 1311

The London Toy & Model Museum
21/23 Craven Hill
London W2 3EN
☎ 071 262 9450/7905

The Teddy Bear Museum
19 Greenhill Street
Stratford-upon-Avon
Warwickshire
CV37 6LF
☎ 0789 293160

INDEX

Acknowledgments

Dorling Kindersley would like to thank the following photographers for their contributions to this book: Jim Coit 1, 2, 3, 4, 5 (top and bottom), 6, 8, 9, 10, 11, 13, 14, 15, 18, 19, 20, 22, 24, 25, 26, 27, 28, 30, 31, 34, 36, 38, 41; Roland Kemp 7, 12, 16, 17, 21, 23, 29, 32, 33, 35, 37, 39.

We would also like to thank the following for their help: Laaren Brown and Susan Thompson for editorial help; Ann Terrell and Sam Grimmer for design assistance; Alastair Wardle and Peter Howlett for their DTP expertise; and Michael Allaby for the index. Our special thanks go to Paul and Rosemary Volpp for their patience and generous contributions to the book.

Border illustrations by Pauline Bayne.
Illustrated letters by Gillie Newman.